Just Another Cheap And Tacky Old Joke Book

Other Books

Stupid Jokes for Clever People
& Clever Jokes for Stupid People

Observations from Another Planet
(Aphorisms & Axioms for the Modern World)

Spaced Out and Cut Up
(Short stories Sci-Fi / Humorous / Horror)

That's the State We're
(Short Stories Science Philosophy & Social Aspects /
Psychology / Emotions)

Empty Thoughts from an Empty Head
(Philosophy / Spirituality)

Logic List English
(Series Work Book)

Logic List English – Vol. 1A
Rhyming Words etc.

Logic List English – Vol. 1B
Spelling Arrangement

Logic List English – Vol. 2A
MULTI-SYLLABLE WORDS

Just Another Cheap And Tacky Old Joke Book

Logic List English – Vol. 2B
MULTI-SYLLABLE WORDS
SPLIT INTO INDIVIDUAL SYLLABLES

Logic List English – Vol. 3
Meaningful Words

Logic List English – Vol. 4A
Phrases & Clauses

Logic List English – Vol. 4B
Phrases & Clauses

Just Another Cheap And Tacky Old Joke Book
By
Tony Sandy*
*Who else would have the cheek to write it?

Published by, DragonEye Publishing

Just Another Cheap And Tacky Old Joke Book

Just Another Cheap And Tacky Old Joke Book
Copyright © 2018, by Tony Sandy

All rights reserved. No part of this book may be reproduced, by any means or in any form whatsoever without written permission from the author and Publisher, except for brief quotation embodied in literary articles or reviews.

Publisher info. Contact
DragonEye Publishing
753A Linden Pl.
Elmira, New York, 14901

For Questions Phone: 1-(607)-333-5256

For information about our books, and for special discounts for single / bulk purchases, please contact DragonEye Publishing Ordering Dept. at:
Website: DragonEyePublishers.com
Email: Orders@DragonEyePublishers.com

To request one of our authors for speaking engagements or book signings, please contact DragonEye Publishing Publicity Dept. at:
Directors@DragonEyePublishers.com

Published by, DragonEye Publishing

ISBN 13: 978-1-61500- 218-4   (Paperback)
ISBN 13: 978-1-61500- 219-1   (EBook)

Library of Congress Control Number: 2018951852

DragonEye Publishing First Edition: July, 2018
First Printing: July 30, 2018

10 9 8 7 6 5 4 3 2 1

Manufactured in the United States of America

Just Another Cheap And Tacky Old Joke Book

Just Another Cheap And Tacky Old Joke Book

Just when you thought it was safe to open another joke book, along comes…

…Stupid Jokes 2!

Just Another Cheap And Tacky Old Joke Book

All Censorship
is Murder
of the Mind – that is
creativity, invention,
insight.
(Talking of which
I could murder
a pint right now).

Just Another Cheap And Tacky Old Joke Book

DEAD-ICATION

This book is dedicated to the late, great Barry Cryer (If he isn't dead yet, this will kill him!)

Just Another Cheap And Tacky Old Joke Book

Just Another Cheap And Tacky Old Joke Book

We just moved into a new place. A guy walked up and introduced himself.
"Hi, I'm Ted, your friendly neighbourhood stalker!"
For some reason my wife slammed the door in his face

I was an event organizer for my local bipolar society but they sacked me, when I took a load of members on a bungee jump. Still can't understand why.

My father is a stone mason - I'm a chip off the old block

Geology is gneiss work, if you can get it

Arsonists just loved the Roaring Twenties!

Three girls were walking down the road. Two were in tears because the third one had just broken up with her boyfriend.
"Don't cry for me Marge and Tina, the truth is I never loved Stew."

The Lord of the jungle visited a churchyard. He introduced himself to one of its residents.
"Yew tree - me Tarzan!"

I bought an electric hedge trimmer the other day but then returned it as I thought what good is it to me when I don't have an electric hedge?

What is Dr Who's favourite car? Well it's not the Mazda

I looked straight into my girlfriend's eyes and said "You're the woman I want to spend some of the rest of my life with." Then she slapped me for some reason.

Frankenstein wanted to prove to his monster how ugly he was, by holding a mirror up to his face but in the end he just couldn't do it as he just didn't have the heart

"Off to work then?"
"Yes, it's a dressing down day, so it's pretty relaxed. You?"
"I'm staying home, it's a dressing gown day, so it's very relaxed"

I lived in America once. When I was there, I went to a yard sale. Trouble was that I only had six inches

I carry my wife's ashes with me wherever I go. I even put out towels for us both when I go to a hotel - his and hearse

I'm getting on a bit, so I asked the bus driver to check that I'd given him the right money.
"No, you're fine. It's correct."
"Thank God, I thought I was getting senile! Still it's nice to know I can still spell"

A man caught me in bed with his wife. He was going to hit me, when I shouted in defense that I was a policeman.
"Where's your uniform then?" he asked
"I'm obviously not wearing it am I? I'm working under cover."

I went to the zoo the other day. There was a sign up
'Warning! Slow Lorris turning'

I disturbed a bird watcher the other day. He was looking a up a tree.
I asked "Is that a long tailed tit?"
"No" he responded "Are you a short tailed twit?"

With all these salted products around nowadays - salted caramel, salted licorice - I thought I'd create my own; salted salt

Opticians going out of business? See if eye care!

I'm not paranoid. I'm just killing time before time kills me!

I asked a cannibal for his daughters hand. He wouldn't give me the rest

Have you lost your idiot child again? That's because a fool and his mummy are soon parted

I know a guy with learning difficulties who's doing rather well at the moment - in fact you could say he's up, even though he's Downs

What's the difference between an Indian city and that part of a military aircraft which carries explosives? One's Bombay, oh and so is the other!

"What's that noise?"
"It's my husband, the dog breeder. I bet he's been bitten by one of the puppies again."
"One hundred and one damnations?"
"I shouldn't doubt it!"

I wasn't happy with the last four star hotel I stayed at - you could see the moon through the roof as well

I separated two eggs the other day. I put one in one room and one in the other, and told them they wouldn't be allowed out until they behaved

My wife and I are arsonists - we get on like a house on fire

"Do you know what B&B owners say about petrochemical workers?"
"No, what?"
"Oily to bed,
Oily to rise
- makes their bed linen
dirty, smelly
and full of crusty pies"

My wife doesn't like her stretch marks. I said, what do you expect when you try to hang yourself?

I dumped my last girlfriend. She was into bondage but I didn't want to get tied down

My wife says wants to be buried in our local cemetery, which I think is a good idea. Of course she doesn't need to be dead at the time

I went to a pet shop sale the other week, looking for a parrot but unfortunately by the time I got there, they'd all flown off the shelves

Do you know why I'm called your step dad?
Yes because you step all over me

If you see Lord Brize-Norton on the shoreline and you want to attract his attention, what do you do? You run down the beach, waving your arms in the air, shouting Sir Brize! Sir Brize!

I walked into a public convenience the other day. It had a sign up saying 'Don't flush hand towels.' I thought how stupid - everyone knows you flush toilets, not hand towels!

I come from a mixed race family - my father runs marathons and my mother is a hurdler

Do people who don't like Charles M Shulz, have a Peanuts allergy?

Two vampires were talking.
'I can't sleep -my wooden box has got a hole in it and all these bugs and beasties keep creeping in! I

can't take it much longer!'
'For a vampire, you've a poor sense of humour'
"I can't help it! Every time I hear a noise, I know it's just another snail in my coffin!'

I bought an electric hedge trimmer the other day but then returned it as I thought what good is it to me when I don't have an electric hedge?

One of the strictly come dancing judges, thought he was going blind, so he went to an optician he knew. "No, you are not going blind my old mate. You are just getting short sighted in your left eye. What I suggest is an old fashioned monocle." 2 weeks later he turned up again.
"Monica!"
"Yes."
"Have you got Mr Goodman's monocle?"
"What?"
"Struth! Is it ready?"
"What?"
"Len's lens!"

The question on every Agatha Christie's fan's lips, about whether one of her more famous characters had used Grecian Two Thousandm has been finally answered. Yes ladies and gentlemen, Lord Edgeware dyes

What do you get if you cross a cleaning cloth with a famous coloured singer and Sean Connery?
Shammy Davis Junior

A butcher had to give up his business because of liver damage – vandals had broken into his shop and trashed the place

A girl joined a rope tying class because she was obsessed with the teacher. One day she caught his attention, after a difficult piece of string manipulation. The rest of the day was spent by her walking around in a daze, going-
"He loves, he loves me knot. He loves me, he loves me knot..."

If you bump into a gorgon, what do you say?
"Stone me!"

Which Scottish regiment, wears extremely unusual headgear?
The Gorgon Highlanders

What monster is thoroughly cheesed off and smells?
Gorgonzola

I'm very spiritual. There's nothing I enjoy more in the evening than settling down with a gin and platonic

Definition of Burns night – fun in the torture chamber

A linguist chased after a cockney.
"Excuse me, you've dropped something!"
"I 'ave?"
Yes, an 'H'.

What do Egyptians shout, when they see somebody running off with ancient artifacts?
"Stop, Thebes!"
How do you know if your car has been approved by the pope?
The engine has been fitted with a catholic convertor
How do you know if a pirate is rich?
If you pull down his trousers, his long-johns are silver, oh ah!

My mummy said I was bad this year, so I'd only be getting one Christmas present – a bag of boiled sweets. Bah, humbugs!

"What do the French do, Pierre?"
"My name's David"
"No, I meant that's what the French do, Pierre"

My wife is seriously into recycling. Last week she put me out with the rubbish but the bin men wouldn't take me

The Flower of Scotland is self-raising

Plugs are a drain on resources
Tapestry is like pastry but made of metal

"Excuse me, have you seen my dog?"
"Dalmation? It's over there."
"Well spotted!"

I had a friend who always wanted to go out on a high, when he retired from his last job. He did. He fell off a skyscraper

"I hear you've got a new guard dog, to protect yourself from zombies?"
"Yes, it's a rottie"

"Get out of my car, you dirty, smelly tramp!"
"But I thought you needed a driver?"
"Don't you know - beggars can't be chauffers"

There are two ways of reacting to an accident – curiosity "I wonder why that happened?" and guilt "Who can I blame for this?"

I visited a chapel of remebrance the other day and spent several moments in deep thought before leaving – and I still can't remember why the hell I went in!

I lowered my colesterol the other day, in one easy step. I moved it from the top shelf to the bottom

Why is it, when we talk to God, it's called praying but when he talks to us, it's called insanity?

"Charlie Wilson as I live and breathe! Oops, I died last week, so I don't do that anymore, do I? Sorry about that!"
I'm not a has-been, I'll have you know, you cheeky so-and-so! (I'm a never was...)

Does a steak have to be well done or medium rare, to kill a vampire?

"That girl's a natural redhead"
"But her hair is orange!"
"No, not her. I mean her friend with the dyed black hair"
My doctor said I was a heavy drinker and it was affecting my health, so I went on a diet

What do you get if you cross a well known Liverpudlian with a well known fish species?
"Look out, it's Cod-cilla!"

Until I saw Baron Frankenstein's surgical team at work, I'd never thought he could put a foot wrong
Quantum physics as a subject is neither here nor there

What do you get if you cross a world famous American author with a world famous Mexican drink?
"Tequilla Mockingbird, senor"

Why is a German in denial, like the UK's emergency number?
They keep repeating 'Nein, nein, nein!"

Just Another Cheap And Tacky Old Joke Book

I went on an intelligence gathering mission to Earth and eventually gathered there wasn't any intelligence

I haven't Eton, which is a Harrowing experience. Personally I blame Westminster (Think I'll get my Winchester and pay them a visit)

I'm not bitter – in fact people think I'm mild mannered but stout hearted, none the less, ready to hop into action at a moments notice. 'That's the spirit!' people shout after me because I don't wine about my situation, even when I face rum conundrums

Being a farmer is harrowing at times. Ploughing through life, keeping stock of my options – until one day I end up planted underground (corny I know but that's my life)

"Here, take this down to the workshop and give it to Scottish Iain, not the English one"
So off the apprentice went
"Are you the Iain with 'I'?'
"No laddie, we've all got two eyes"

I'm a kept man, despite my wife desperately trying to give me away
I went to a funeral at a crematorium last week "Smoking or non-smoking?" the attendant asked

I'm not depressed – Mahmood is good!

Familiarity breeds attempt

Ken Wood is a mixer!

I'm a bored again Christian

Illiteracy is a four letter word

I live in an altered State – California

After reading The Grapes Of Wrath, I got drunk and discovered the wrath of grapes

I'm never out of the doctor's office, since I caught hyperchondria
A man appeared on Mastermind, where he refused to answer questions on his specialist subject of Patrick McGoohan's TV series, The Prisoner

Two musical instruments were talking, when a third joined them. After a while the new one left. "Why did you tell him you weren't married, when you are? Oh, you're such a lyre!"

I went to a play about Zen the other day. It was poorly received, with only one handclapping

The reason the Chinese are so slim is that they're all on the Lo Fat diet

Cannibals believe that a Martian a day, helps you work, rest and play
In Nursery Land, Humpty-Dumpty was viciously attacked and left for dead. Police said he was beaten to within an inch of his life

Mr and Mrs Wright wanted to have a Chinese baby couldn't produce one – proving two Wrights don't make a Wong

A monkey could make the same mess on canvas Jackson Pollock did. The only difference is that it couldn't ride a bicycle

A farmer was arrested today, when it was discovered that when he called his wife a cow, it wasn't an insult but a fact

Humpty-Dumpty was confirmed as the lead in a new production of Shakespeare's 'Omlette, Prince of Denmark'

The war on drugs is all going to pot

Humpty-Dumpty is a great big oeuf!

Donald Duck is a quack!

The Mind is an I-Cloud

I'm intolerant of intolerance!
Seen on a garment - 'I don't wear t-shirts like this'

Cheap cocaine is not to be sniffed at

People who take cocaine, get right up my nose!

I'm twisted!! (Too screwed, to screw)

Americans have a right to bare arms (and bare legs if they want)

I wash my hands of people with OCD

As a drunk I'm an honorary member of The Flat Earth Society

In speedos, nobody can hear you scream

Welsh drunks – keep calm and carry Owen

UB40 and IB50!

Electrical engineers know that resistance is useless
Every time I hear the word
Cull-
Colch-
Ciltch-
I reach for my dictionary

Ignorant people won't take know for an answer

The only thing that never changes, is change because it is always changing

It used to be that the law had to be seen, to be done. Nowadays it's obscene and you get done!
He who cuts corners, ends up going round in circles

Is that a nut that can be seen through the keyhole? Hey, no Pecan!

Why are the small minded, invariably big headed?
In Venice it's a doge eat doge world

Help, I'm drowning in a stream of consciousness!

Equality! Fraternity! Liberace!

College drop-out (Poison Ivy League)

It has rained so much lately that we had to get rid of the dog. We've got a pet slug now

I asked my wife if would mind me painting her. She said no, so I poured a tin of gloss over her head

Just Another Cheap And Tacky Old Joke Book

The Exorcist – still turning heads after all these years

Microsoft have developed a new font specifically for doctors, which is why only they can read it

A new male nurse at a care home, introduced himself to one of the residents. As he was walking away, the guy shouted after him
'Hey Andy, what's your name again?'
I saw a really disgusting sight the other day – a dog licking its anus horribilis

Feeling a little run down? Then get off the bloody road you idiot!

I'm world famous! (in my own mind anyway)

I got into the Christmas spirit early this year but my wife caught me, and made me put the bottles back into the cupboard

Everytime I hear the word culture, I reach for my microscope
Do my testicles look big in this?

Just Another Cheap And Tacky Old Joke Book

Out of my mind – back in five minutes

I was carrying my wife, Penelope, across a stream when I suddenly thought 'I don't have to do this' and that's when the penny dropped

I thought the British were liberal but I was wrong. I went to a dinner party the other day and the host said 'Feel my guest,' so I did and she slapped me

If I ruled the world, it would be covered in lines

I was keen to help Baron Frankenstein with his work, until he told me, it would cost me an arm and a leg

I'm all in favour of capital punishment but I don't see why lower case letters shouldn't be punished as well

I think I've got hyperchondria – is there a cure?

Lung disease? TB or not TB, that is the question!

Just Another Cheap And Tacky Old Joke Book

If it's not Baroque, don't fix it

Somebody once said that I was a master of my craft. Trouble is it was a sinking ship

I tried to help a girl off the streets the other day. She was totally ungrateful.
"Now how am I going to get home – that was the last bus, you idiot!"

Tutankhamun is a mummys boy
During World War Two, Britain had a squadron of eggheads, who were poached from the intelligence corps, some were hard boiled and some soft but they all scrambled when the orders were given

When I was first a nurse it was considered a vocation. Nowadays girls are so bone idle, it is considered a vacation

A priest fell from grace yesterday. Photographers burst into the room where he was having an affair with her and he fell out the window

A young lad joined the paleontology department of The Natural History Museum. On his first day he was asked to collect some dinosaur remains from

the basement storage section.
"I've been sent to collect the three horned dinosaur bones"
"Triceratops"
Okay, where is she?"

Two schoolboys were talking
"I think my PE teacher has a super body"
"No, she's Miss-shapen'

I think that idea that humour is funny, is laughable

When I became an optician, I never realised how busy I'd become – in fact up to my eyes in it, every night

There are real advantages to being Henry the Eighth's executioner. When I retired I got really good severance pay

How do you know if you've found a container for a Glaswegian's glasses?
It will be a hard case

Just say no to drugs and yes, yes, yes to sex!
A train pulled into a station and immediately fell to pieces. It was chuffed to bits

Just Another Cheap And Tacky Old Joke Book

Scotland – land of the midge-night sun
"Oh look, over there is Portland Bill!"
"Yes, and over there is Southampton Sal!"

I had a subway sandwich once. Never again. It must have been lying in the underpass for weeks

A sentry jumped to attention.
"Halt, who goes there?"
"That's right, it's me – Hugo. How did you recognize me from that distance?"
The grand old Duke of York had manic depression. When he was up, he was up and when he was down, he was down, and when he was only half way up, he lived quite a normal life

A cafe in London is giving free coffee to breast feeding mothers but they have to provide their own milk

When I moved to Australia, it was a night of wine, women and so-long.

A famous comedian visited an Incontinent charity's HQ, to do a gig. By the time he'd come to the end of his routine, there wasn't a dry thigh in the entire place

The Gerof eagle is almost extinct. This is because every time the male bird tries to have his wicked way with a female, she screams 'Gerof!'

A lynch mob from The South chased a man into a factory, where he tripped and fell into a vat full of boiling oil. This was the start of Kentucky Fried Chicken

A young lad was fed up being bare-chested. So his dad said he could fix it. He took him down to the meadow behind the house, in March. He got him to lay down and said, don't move.
"This is guaranteed to put hares on your chest, son"

Why is it that when I wear my wellies and I go uphill, my socks go downhill?

I am what you'd call an alternative comedian. If you want an alternative to comedy, that's me!

I prefer M&S, to S&M (or do I?)

Just Another Cheap And Tacky Old Joke Book

Nuclear war is a load of ballistics

I understand you and your brother are identical?
Which one of you is the twin?

"Were I come from, we'd say about a bloke like that he was as friendly as arsenic and poisonous as jam"
"Where do come from then?"
"The lunatic asylum up the road"

The modern day version of Richard the Third
"A Ford, a Ford – my kingdom for a Ford!"

Rene Descartes reborn in the modern age
I think therefore I spam

'Mum can I play in the field behind the house?'
'No, it's dangerous'
'I don't care, I'm going!'
'Well if you stand on a landmine, don't come running to me'

I wish I hadn't married a loose woman - she fell to bits on the honeymoon
Champion limbo dancers are the lowest of the low

I hate it when Baron Frankenstein gets the upper hand. It means he has got enough body parts to make another monster, to chase me with

I used to work in a laundry until my colleagues hung me out to dry

What is the opposite of a manhole cover?

By the time I got to the top of the hill, my legs were like jelly, the sun cream had on my nose had melted and water was running off my brow like a wet sponge. No wonder I felt a trifle tired
I played Russian roulade once. It was like Russian roulette but they used poison cake slices instead of bullets

Two shellfish were talking
'Mike got lucky last night'
'Oh yeh?'

'Yeh, he pulled a mussel'

I saw an elderly actress who couldn't act the other day - mutton dressed as ham

A friend had a cold
I said do you want a sweet?
He said it might help
What sort I asked?
'A-chew!'
'Alright - no need to shout!'
As a professional arsonist I really appreciate the authorities creating fire assembly points

And the lion will lay down with the lamb but only after it's eaten one or two sheep

'That Freud is a fraud, a quack!'
'What do you mean?'
'I told him that I wanted to kill my father and sleep with my mother, and he believed me!'

Joe Green was in court, over royalties not paid to him by the opera house.

'Now Mr Green, please can you tell the jury how much you've been paid for your work?'

'Figure-o, figure-o, figure-o!'

'I hear Charlie Sheen is HIV'
'Are you positive?'
' No but he is!'
'I went to a town where the food was foul'
'Nuneaton?'
'You bet!'

Richard Bach has written a follow up to one of his most famous books - it's called Jonathan Livingston Sequel

From all of us budding stand up comedians, to our audiences: We who are about to dry salute you!

Is someone who works for Cadburys, a glass and a half full type person?

'Sergei stop being so uppity! Remember without me you are nothing more than a mere-cat!'

'I am not coming out!'
'But it's okay to be gay nowadays'
'I don't care!'

Just Another Cheap And Tacky Old Joke Book

'Alright but it's just cupboard love'

Did you hear about the sexist, who complained he was being treated by a woman because it was Guys Hospital?

As a proud zombie I can hold my head up, even when decapitated

When I was a kid all girls wanted for Christmas was My Little Pony. Nowadays all little boys want is My Little Droney

'I am willing to die for my beliefs!'
'What do you believe in then?'
'Nothing, I'm a nihilist'

Why was the botoxed, bleached blond with implants disqualified from the race?
She made a false start

I love home baking - that's why I've been an arsonist for 30 years

What does the moaner in the fabric colouring plant say every morning?
'We're all going to dye!'

I used to work round the clock when I was younger.
I really hated dusting

I climbed a cliff face yesterday. Cliff wasn't too happy about it though
When on a visit to France I was asked what I thought about the Burghers of Calais.
I replied 'Nice, if well done between fresh gaps

I'm so unlucky that when I went to a wife swapping party, all I got in exchange was a potted plant

My wife has blood vessels showing through her tights. She tried getting rid of them but it was all in vein

I played hide and seek with a zombie. He hid behind a curtain but you could see his feet. It was a dead give away

Why did the householder throw a bucket of hot water over the rent collector?
He didn't like cold callers
What did the electrical engineer say when a river got in his way?
'Dam you!'

Just Another Cheap And Tacky Old Joke Book

The British Prime Minister was asked if he had a place in his cabinet for an old enemy
'Yes, stuffed and in the one by the door'

Why did the chicken cross the toad? Because he was afraid he wouldn't get his cut from the robbery

My wife makes such weak tea that it tastes like watered down water

I call my wife The BBC because she keeps repeating the same things, over and over again

A shoplifter who only stole washing up liquid, was pursued by an assistant but he couldn't catch her as she was away with the fairies

Two people were at a train station, saying goodbye
'I will give you a ring next time I am in town'
'Does that mean we are engaged?'

I saw something weird the other day – a shutter hand-in-hand with another shutter. It was a case of the blinds leading the blinds

I used to know a really dodgy drug dealer. He always dealt from the bottom of the deck

As soon as I jumped into bed, my head sunk into the pillow but that is the trouble with leaky water beds

I have got the body of a twenty year old. The police still have not found out where I buried him

I bought an electric toothbrush. Pointless - I don't have electric teeth

When the Beggar's Opera was first performed, it was poorly received by the rich

All the animals in the Chinese bear enclosure started a custard pie fight. By the time the keepers got in it was pandemonium

An electrician working on a light fitting, over a deep fat fryer, slipped and fell in. He was battered to death

I love The Ring Cycle. It's my favourite washing machine setting

Cannibals like nothing better than a little nan with their curries

I had a serious medical complaint when I was younger. The doctor said that if I didn't stop pestering him, he would call the police

Just Another Cheap And Tacky Old Joke Book

Two men were on a golf.

'Here, have a snort - it will help you relax'

'For heaven's sake! I have told you before - I don't believe in drinking and driving'

'I went to a strange hairdresser the other day. He cut great chunks out of my hair, indiscriminately, sprayed my head with curry, then gave me an alcoholic cake covered in chocolate sprinkles.'
'Rum baba?'
'He sure was!'

A sheriff's posse caught a handful of rustlers, putting nooses round their necks and mounting them on their horses.
'Okay men, when I give you the signal, give me a high five'

What do you shout if someone runs off with two letters of the alphabet?
'A, U!'

In the UK we have wall to wall carpets. In Berlin they have wall to wall, wall

My girlfriend has the girl next door looks. In fact she is the girl next door
'Guess what Algie, I am going on a diet! Chocs away!'

How did the generous cannibal confuse his friend? He ran down the road, shouting 'I've got a bone to pick with you!'

Everybody forgets Whisky Galore's subtitle - Scotch on the Rocks

A karate expert walked into a DIY store and smashed all the woodwork between him and the assistant, using his iron fist. Police are treating it as a terror-wrist, counter attack

The doctor sent me to the hospital with a letter. The 'P' had fallen off the sign

My next door neighbours accused our dog of eating their feline, so we were forced to take it to the vets for a catscan

Just Another Cheap And Tacky Old Joke Book

Why is it pointless telling a nun, a sex joke?
They just don't get it

Amateur ventriloquists – Gottle-o-gear, no idea!

I saw somebody I knew the other day. He shouted across to me, do you want a lift? I said, no thank you – I live in a bungalow

Did you know Cambidge University has connections to the Mafia? That is why it is full of Dons.

Since my uncle fell into a cement mixer, he's become set in his ways

Every time I ask anybody a question, they say Hugh knows but why the hell doesn't he tell me!

My wife asked me to look at a date on the calendar. I said, it's not a date, it's a sultana

I don't know why people think I'm an addict – just because I take pills with my pils

I tried to find the source of the Nile but the bottle was well hidden

'Which do you prefer, a thoroughbred or a mongrel?'
'A cat'

Frankenstein has become so good at making monsters for people that he is now offering part exchange on older models

A husband and wife were watching gymnastics on television.
'I couldn't do that!'
'Piece of cake'
'Do you mean you could?'
'No, I just want a piece of cake'
'I've just converted to Islam'
'Funny that – I've just converted to gas'

We've been plagued by zombies recently, going round banging on doors in the middle of the night. It's got so bad that we had to put up a notice - 'No Cold Callers'

Count Dracula came to see me the other day. He didn't stay long – it was just a flying visit

Just Another Cheap And Tacky Old Joke Book

I tried to get my friend to overcome his fear of snakes, by getting him to pick up a rattler. Unfortunately he couldn't grasp the situation

People who think they don't make mistakes, are making a mistake
I had a misspent youth. I spent it with my teacher, Miss Spence

'I visited a friend in hospital the other week. He's in a high dependency unit'
'ICU?'
'Yes and I see you but what the hell has that got to do with it?'

I saw a sign in the high street the other day. It said, 'Janson's – criminal lawyers' and I thought aren't they all?

Two dry biscuits jump into the back of a taxi and start giggling hysterically. The driver turns round and says, you two must be crackers!

I M 1 – R U 1 2? By the way R U 3 4 T?

When they are in GB, The BeeGees give me the heebie-jeebies!

On a visit to Britain, The UK was KO'd by the KKK, OK?

I see some boffin has reinvented anthrax? I wonder, should he be done for plaguerism?

Who won the rowing contest at the fruit olympics? The coxless pippins of course!

I went for a colonic irrigation last Saturday. The girl who carried it out had an unusual name – Dinah Rod

I joined a chain gang when I visited America. It was a ground breaking experience

You need to get rid of that hoover – it's a death trap! Every time you use it, you're Dyson with death

The trouble with being a female flower is that you can guarantee you'll be stalked

The police were searching for an escaped criminal, who was hiding in Billingsgate fish market. Suddenly an officer spotted him.
'Okay Johnston, come on out – you're under a wrasse'

When Baron Frankenstein said he wanted to pick my brains, I didn't realise that he meant it literally!

I asked a ventriloquist's dummy to name a famous Scotsman and he mentioned somebody I had never heard of – Yogurt The Goose.

I've got two friends – one is nutty in a fruity kind of way and the other is fruity in a nutty kind of way

Being a farmer is like being a witch – it's all hubble, stubble; toil and trouble
I went to medical school in order to train as a surgeon but my tutor said I wasn't cut out for it

I'm in a class of my own – the teacher hates me

My wife says she wants me to be in a committed relationship but as I told her I've already been committed once and I didn't like it

A well known bank robber has just released his autobiography – it's called 'From blags to riches'

Frankenstein loves his monster to bits – which is why he has to keep sewing it back together again

All British prime ministers have a Chequered past

A preying mantis and his wife were arguing
"Okay, okay! Don't bite my head off!"

No Bill, when I said I wanted access to the car, I didn't mean hit it with axes, you idiot!

Shakespeare went to Scotland to support his favourite football team. Watching them get slaughtered by the opposition, he walked out halfway through, muttering to himself 'Partick is such sweet sorrow'

British sitcoms? Makes you want to ask – Steptoe and son, are you being served porridge?

Frankenstein started off experimenting with small animals. In fact he could often be seen in the garden, working on his self-assembly kits

An elderly lady walks up to a council road sweeper, squints and looks inside his dust cart.
"What a lovely baby but I think it needs a bath and its nappy changed"

Just Another Cheap And Tacky Old Joke Book

Got a headache? Who should you visit for instant relief? Doctor Frankenstein – it's a no brainer

An overweight cat with a ravenous appetite, swallowed a waterfowl, whole. An acquaintence turned to his friends and said in a mocking tone "Oh look, it's a duck filled fatty pus!"

A man obsessed with playing football, had an ultimatum from his wife – either get rid of of all your paraphanalia or I'm leaving you. So he did what he was told, only to catch his wife in bed with another man.
"I burst my balls for you and this is how you repay me!"

007 got stuck in a traffic jam, so knew he couldn't make it to an important meeting with M. He immediately texted Miss Moneypenny, signing off with 'From rush hour with love'

During the winter, every time the weather changed for the worse, Julius Caesar would collapse with an epileptic fit. This led to the warning going out, whenever the sky darkened "Hail-seizure!"

A girl into martial arts and rock climbing, was surprised at home by a friend, who caught her her collecting stamps. She immediately collapsed onto the floor in Anna-philately shock.

If you're addicted to your computer, is it a terminal illness?

Gangsters start off their bedtime stories with the words 'Once upon a crime...'

Two rival biologists were in The Amazon, hunting for new species, when one of them noticed a small amphibian
"That's minute!"
The other one snatched it back
"No, it's my newt!"

I've a friend who hates telling lies. Everytime that he tells a fib, he has a fit and collapses onto the ground. He's what you might call a convulsive liar

A miser in the eighteenth century, who intended to take all his money with him when he died, saw a sweet by the side of the road and bent down to pick it up, just as a coach crashed into the pavement, sending part of it flying off down the street and killng him. His lawyer described it is as his clients lost wheel and tasty-mint

Beggar 'Alms for the poor!'
Passerby, turning to his companion 'And legs for the weak, I should imagine'

Two wealthy Texans were talking about how they acquired their money. One was reticent to say and turned to walk off, slipped and fell into some sticky liquid.
"So you're in oil then?"

People from The Highlands of Scotland never smile – they're afraid of getting frostbite of the teeth

I went to The Citizens Advice Bureau for advice – they advised me to become a citizen

A garlic bread a day keeps the vampires away

What's another name for a kilt?
A ballgown
I'm Frankenstein's right hand man but I've no idea where he is going to get the left hand one from

I had a toothache, so I went to the dentist. He tried kidding me, to take my mind off what he was doing but was so distracted he took out the wrong tooth by mistake, so I said pull the other one!

When I was in the crab army, I was always getting caught in pincer movements

People who want to pump their lips with botox, deserve a fat lip and a thick ear

I wonder if President Putin will cry-me-a river over the Ukraine?

I worked in The Museum of Moder Art, where I discovered a particular art movement. You could say my MOMA is my Dada

I have a zombie who helps me in the garden. I use him because I know he has green fingers

What is a torturer's favourite card game?
Snap!

Two concert organisers were having trouble deciding what to exclude from their respective anniversary concerts for a particular composer. In the end, one of them turned to the other and said "Tell you what, I'll scratch your Bach, if you scratch mine"

I asked a zombie to cast an eye over my garden – big mistake, it got stuck in a tree

Manchester is sexist town – it should be Personchester
"Dad can you tell me another bedtime tale?"
"No, we live in a bungalow – you can only have a single storey"

One of the cast of The Archers lost his temper and stomped out of the studio. He took Ambridge at the producers comments

I pulled into a transport cafe. It was at a T-junction. I didn't go in – I wanted coffee

A surgeon put on their gown and walked into the theatre, then ran out embarrassed – it was a musical theatre
Another surgeon put on their mask and gown, before entering the theatre. The usher turned round and said
"The masked ball is next door madam"

There are two types of people in the world – those who shooy first and ask questions later and those who get shot while asking questions

A strange, out of place creature was found on the Scottish coast. A journalist asked the zoologist involved in identifying it, if it was a plant?
"Oh no, it is definitely an animal"

"Waiter there's a fly in my soup!"
"If you were to sit down, the zip would automatically come out of your broccoli and stilton, sir"

"Listen to the music – it is the children of the night!"
"Well get out of bed, it's your turn to change the twins nappies'

"Look at that! No parking on the street, yet that family have cars for the parents and both kids, parked on the road. Disgusting!"
"I agree – silly four cars"

If wealth is an addiction, is cold turkey it's only cure?

Just Another Cheap And Tacky Old Joke Book

I saw a man cutting small, furry creatures in half. I said what the hell do you think you're doing? He replied, it might be this or it might be that. Look, I said, stop splitting hares

I was going to mention a joke about Thmas Crapper but I think lavatorial jokes are a tad overdone

Two old codgers were talking about their ultimate demise.
"Tell you what, if I can come to your funeral, you can come to mine"

I thought a UK comedian was a good guy until recently, then I discovered the true colours of Ben Elton!

A petrol pump nozzle said to a diesel engine "Okay, don't move or I'll fill you full of unleaded!"

As a drunk I believe in carpet diem – seize the floor

I forgot Remembrance Sunday

A member of the local gentry in Wales, was surprised by a well known local scoundrel, when he jumped out in front of him
"Good heavens – it's bad Evans!"

I robbed a bank the other day – got away with a tin of beans and a potato (it was a food bank)

My wife and me have a joint account, so we don't run out of cannabis

My dog has eaten so much jelly that it has got the collie wobbles

Did you hear about the drunk who went cold turkey on alcohol? Eventually he lost it with his wife nagging him about being bad tempered, since he came off the booze, that he attacked and killed her. He was charged with thirst degree murder

A famous viking king was renowned for his drinking. From that point on, any ruler who followed him into power, who couldn't hold their drink, was known as being drunk as a Canute

Just Another Cheap And Tacky Old Joke Book

Granny Smith is the apple of my eye

Celery – what people from Edinburgh get paid instead of wages
What do cannibals call Christians?
Happy meals
I read an interesting book the other day. It was called bouncing back from a bullet wound, by Rick O'Shea

How does a miser measure time?
By using Greenwich 'mean' time

Never keep a werewolfas a pet – it always bites the hand that feeds it

A stockbroker was walking with a friend, who heard him say 'Sell, sell – buy, buy!' then throw down his mobile phone.
'What was that all about?'
"Bloody cell phone wouldn't work, so I tried to explain to my wife, shouted goodbye then smashed the thing in frustration!'

We have a rather smelly old bear as a pet – we call it Winnie the pooh
Little Jimmy came running home crying. His mother

asked him what was wrong.
"We went round old man Jenkins house and said trick or treat. He said trick and squirted us in the face with a water cannon."

I heard my wife on the phone the other day. Every so often she'd say "
Surely not!"
In the end I asked her what was going on.
"Bad news?"
"No, I was just talking to that woman with a wicked sense of humour, Shirley Knott."

"I've taught my pet duck to lay the table."
"Pity, mine can only lay eggs."

"The enemy don't know how few of us there are sergeant."
"No sir."
"Do you think we should continue to deceive them or withdraw overnight?"
"You mean trick or retreat?"

In cyberspace nobody can eat your icecream.

"Captain, we've just found another body in the bakery"
"Don't tell me, it's another John Dough."

What do you say to a paleontologist at lunch time?
"Tea, Rex?"

I asked Baron Frankenstein if he needed a hand. He said no thanks but if I knew where he could get a spare leg, he would be much obliged.

America and Britain are uniting to form a super state. The rest of the world is utterly dismayed at this. The union will be known as U-SUK.

If there are two holes in the road, which one does a Spanish bullfighter fill first - hole B or hole A?

A man and his wife were arguing about his lack of backbone.
"What do you mean, grow some nuts? My name isn't Jimmy Carter!"

My wife says I'm autistic - I want everybody to hold me in awe.

How do you handle explosive Welsh cheese?
Caerphilly.

Two men were talking. One said he'd had six weeks off when his mother died.
The other thought about this and said
"How long do you think you would have got off, if you'd died?"
When I was younger women threw themselves at me. Trouble was most of them missed.

"What the hell happened to your shades?"
"We couldn't afford Venetian blinds, so I had the brilliant idea of getting a blind Venetian to put them up instead."

A man was in hospital with his seriously ill wife.
"Don't you die on me Mary Lou or I will never speak to you again!"
When I joined the police, I was sent to the dog handling branch but as I couldn't see it when I looked up the tree, I went home.

I made an expanded polystyrene statue of my girlfriend.
She said
"Foam me? You shouldn't have!"

Just Another Cheap And Tacky Old Joke Book

My dog chases balls. He's non into bitches.

Do sword swallowers eat a staple diet?
One flea asked another flea why he hadn't seen him lately.
"I've been on Olly Day haven't I"

Home games - leap Carl and carry Tom.

My wife thinks she is a car. She keeps asking me to back her up.

Why didn't Schubert finish his symphony, even though his mother asked him to?
He wasn't hungry.

I have got a robot friend, who comes from the poor part of town. He lives in a zinc estate.I

I told my boss that I had served time behind bars. He wasn't impressed - especially when I couldn't name any of the pubs I had worked in.

My dog eats bricks. It has eaten us out of house and home.

Parents, are your children stuck in front of the TV or computer screen? Then you need to get them on 'Failed Activity Teenager' course or F.A.T. program.

To women were talking about their Indian neighbours.
"Do they speak English?"
"Urdu, he doesn't."

Mickey, you're not a cop anymore. You'll never make it as a lift operator, if you keep freaking out people by telling them, you're taking them down.

Two dogs were talking.
"People don't like my owner."
"Why is that - he seems nice enough to me?"
"Well he is a whistleblower isn't he."

I am a useless boxer. I sting like a butterfly and fly like a bumblebee.

A man rushed into a removals company and pulled out a gun.
"Okay, nobody moves!"

Just Another Cheap And Tacky Old Joke Book

A hippie became sherrif of a frontier town. Putting a rope round a gunslingers neck, he said "Hang loose man!"

As a baker, I act as a roll model for my kids.

If a vampire invites you to lunch, what do you say?
"No fangs."
Cambridge Dons are known as the cardie nostra.

I moved into temporary accommodation yesterday. As I walked through the door, the owner gave me a plank. I asked what it was for.
"It's bed and board isn't it."

Glaswegians are hard to Govan.

"Farms are dangerous places, you know, Charlie! Lookout - Cow! hide! Duck!"
"You chicken!"

I never pay any attention to what the weatherman says - he has got his head in the clouds.

A man came up to me the other day and whispered in my ear.
"I have got a contagious disease - pass it on."

Just Another Cheap And Tacky Old Joke Book

I know a doctor, who had to give up his practice. His patients made him sick.

I have been making coats filled with feathers for years. It is a depressing job. In fact it is no exaggeration to say that I have been feeling down for a long while.

And now ladies and gentlemen, performing his latest hit - it's Neil Down and 'Pray.'

I hate begging letters, especially at Christmas. I told my wife I am not divorcing her and that's that!

I am a werewolf - I can't bear lambs wool close to my skin.
I visited the red light district once but I didn't stay long. It turned green.

A group of dead comedians were in heaven, waiting to get reborn. Talk drifted onto the subject of reincarnation.
"Who remembers the last time they died?"
"I do. It was the Glasgow Empire."

My wife bought me a memory stick, for my fiftieth birthday. Every time I forget something important,

she hits me with it.
Courtroom scene: "President Putin, I put it to you that you were complicit in the murder of Alexander Litvinenko."
"Nyet"
"I further put it to you that your government lent Ukrainian rebels the missile system that brought down Malaysian flight MH17."
"Nyet"
I must also put it to you that your government deliberately interfered with the American elections, through computer hacking."
"Nyet"
"Are you lying about all these accusations?"
"Nyet...my conscience is trying to tell me something...."

I never knew I was pregnant until I went into Labour during the last elections

As an atheist comedian, I expect to have a humorist wedding

I work as a prison guard and one guy signed to me that he was innocent and shouldn't be facing execution. I said, then why are you on deaf row?

There are so many actors with the same name in Hollywood that the Oscar's committee is chartering a special plane to bring them all in - Ryan Air.

Military commanders are not very bright. They only possess general knowledge

In the winter, the only day of the week I really enjoy is Thawsday

"Mummy, what do you call the raisins that come out of a deer's behind?""
"I don't know."
"Hind's baked beans."

I woke up with my hands and feet bound and large rocks tied to both of them as well. I turned my head towards my wife and said, this isn't exactly what I meant, when I said that I wanted to be 'weighted' on hand and foot.

When me and the wife have sex, she moans a lot. "The ceiling still hasn't been painted. Did you lock the front door? When are you going to weed the front garden?"

Just Another Cheap And Tacky Old Joke Book

My guru was not happy with my progress as a student, so he sent me for an 'I' examination.

"Have you packed everything?"
"I think so, but you always forget something don't you?"
"What is the capital of Turkey?"
"I don't know. There, I told you I would forget something!"

Tom Hanks is suffering from a mystery illness but his doctor just thinks it is a Da Vinci cold.

My husband was angry that I went for a waxing. In the end he tore me off a strip.
I wanted to learn how to operate a guillotine, so I went for a job interview. Unfortunately I arrived late and was told that I had missed the cut off point.

The unfairness of life! I haven't been named and shamed for a crime I committed but blamed and framed, for one I didn't do!

The jury is split on whether a famous singer from the sixties, is guilty of murder or not - it's a real Cliff hanger.

Police investigating the Schrödinger cat murder, say it is an open and shut case.
Do you know what the height of ignorance is?
Six foot, two.

I don't like Bakewell anymore - it's full of tarts

A removals company was helping a doctor move house, when one of the men wanted to ask him about an old injury.
"Take a seat, I'll be with you in a minute."

Scotland's national bard had two brothers. The eldest was a bible basher and the youngest tried to follow in his brothers' footsteps but wasn't talented enough. They were known as severe and superficial Burns.

A man walks into a hairdressers.
"I would like a composers haircut."
"What's that?"
"A short Bach and sides."

A cockerel was trying to teach a chicken to drive but she insisted on taking her kids along. Eventually the exasperated instructor, fed up with the noise and antics, said, I want you to put your foot on the accelerator and let the clutch out.

What do thirsty umpires at Wimbledon shout? "Juice! Miss Barker to serve."

If you drop toast into Schrödinger's box, does it land butter side up?

"What's that horrifically dressed thing stumbling towards us?"
"Don't you know? That's Frumpenstein's monster!"

If you get cream from a creamery, do you get dreams from a dreamery?

Notice above the entrance to IKEA: Abandon trolleys, all who enter here

The trouble with being a cubist is that you always end up painting yourself into a corner

What's the difference between a famous TV doctor and a well known UK serial killer? One is Doctor Kildare and the other is doctor dare kill.

A man was visiting Donald Trump's African wildlife park, when he noticed none of the animals were

moving, so he went up to one and poked it.
"Typical! Trust Trump to promote fake gnus!"
What do you call Sponge Bob Square Pants cousin?
Wedgie

Why are useless criminals no good at shaving?
Because they are always getting nicked

Two tadpoles were talking, when one let out a startled cry.
"What the hell is that over there!"
"Nice try but you can't fool me - I wasn't spawn yesterday!"

I will always help a lady in distress but not dat-tress because I don't like the colour or style.

We all know Humpty Dumpty had a great fall but what was his summer like?

My old dog is on its last legs. It's worn out fifteen pairs already.

Why are the Welsh never picked as spies?
Because of all the leeks
What do you call a zombie underwater?
Dead man, snorkeling

Two zombies were talking, when a third one walked passed, dressed in pink trousers, an orange jacket and a hat with flowers in it.
"Trust Russell! Personally I wouldn't be seen dead dressed like that!"

After the explosion, the police carried out a finger tip search but only found legs and arms.
My wife demanded breakfast in bed, then had the cheek to complain about the eggs and bacon, poured all over the sheets.

The only thing certain about the future is that there is nothing certain about the future.

I know a botanist, who was useless at his job but thankfully he has turned over a new leaf.

Amateur brewers - all the beer, no idea!

My wife says I dance like Astaire - stiff as a bannister.

I am going out with a woman who works for an electricity company. She is what you would call my current girlfriend.

An former vice president, who was into jazz, decided to start up his own band. He called it The Al Gore Rhythm.

Billy Connolly was walking down the street, in his famous blow-up banana boots, when he stood on some tin tacks that somebody had accidentally dropped. Immediately he popped his cloggs.
I wish that I had never married a horse. Everyday it's just nag, nag, nag.

My brother-in-law was a lookout on a boat, smuggling drugs for the Mafia. He was found kipping with the kippers, so now he is permanently sleeping with the fishes.
I used to be a paperboy, until Geppetto turned me into a real boy.

I had problems with every single woman I married, until I found a permanent solution for all of them - sulphuric acid (don't be vague, ask for Haig).

God's vacuum cleaner wasn't working very well, so he called in a repair man.
"What's wrong with it?"
"Jehovah's broken."

He was only a scientists son but he knew what Ellie meant.

Two rival classical record collectors were arguing about mutual sabotage, aimed at stopping the other one getting hold of rare and valuable editions. Finally they called a truce.
"Right, I won't scratch your Bach, if you won't scratch mine."

What do you say to a condiment, when it leaves the table?
Tartar sauce!
At the world Scrabble championships, The British captain was giving a pep talk to his team
"Okay lads, when you go out there, I want you to give them -L"

I bumped into somebody the other day. He said watch where you are going! I looked but I couldn't see any watch.

I found myself in a prisoner of war camp. It was so frightening, it made the Herr's stand up on the back of my neck.

What do you tie memories up with? A forget-me-knot

I picked up a really belligerent hitchhiker the other day. In the end I told him where to get off.

"I ran up a hill yesterday."
"Fell running?"
"No, I managed to stay upright."

Men's main complaint about sex is that they do all the work and women do all the moaning.

A man walks into an electrical store.
"I would like a Bridget Jones fridge-freezer please."
"What do you mean? "
"One with big drawers."

I walked into a bar the other day and jumped back in surprise.
"You're the double of my wife's brother!"
"Double?"
"That's kind of you. Whisky please!"

Just Another Cheap And Tacky Old Joke Book

I am never going to use Harry Potter's invisible mending service ever again. I still can't find my coat.

Misers go to singles bars. The more generous go to doubles bars.

I am a sewage worker for the council. My wife is depressed, my daughter complains all the time. You could say my life consists of whining women and pong.

Why is Jane Austin considered a petrol head? Because she has always got her head stuck under a bonnet.

My neighbour was ill so I took his dog out for a walk. When I got back my wife asked what it was called. I said I took it for a walk, not to talk to it.

"You look terrible mate - what's wrong with you?"
"I have got King Arthur's insomnia. "
"What's that then?"
"Sleepless Knights syndrome."

A war developed between flying insects and crawling ones, which didn't turn out well for one

side...
"My lord I regret to inform you that your flies are undone and worse than that, you've got ants in your tanks."

My cousin drives a taxi, cleans windows and is a tree surgeon but excels in sewage work. In fact he is known as a Jack of all trades but a master of dung.

I know a company that deals in stolen Egyptian artifacts. Their motto is complete satisfaction or your mummy back.

I parked my car on the putting green, after carrying out a wheel spin across the grass. The groundsman went nuts. So I said keep your hair on, it's a driving range after all.

My uncle shaves his head and doesn't believe in keeping his trousers up with anything but a belt. He's got no hairs and braces.

My father was a member of a secret society - so secret, he wasn't even sure he'd joined.

I wanted to talk to my doctor about erectile

dysfunction but unfortunately it didn't come up in conversation.

"I see your car has broken down. Do you belong to the AA?"
"No, the II"
"What's that?"
"A local break down service, which comes to collect me and the guy says:-
"Aye, aye - I see you've still got that broken down old wreck of a car then?"

A trapeze artist was wheeled into casualty.
"What happened to you?"
"My boss said I wasn't any good at my job and he was going to have to let me go - and he did, literally."

In a pub the rule is thirst come, thirst served.

Hans Zimmer was framed.

I was worried about taking my first dose of LSD, so I visited Trip Advisor.

I'm so tired, I don't even have the energy to lie down.

An angry neighbour stuck their head over the fence as I was mowing the lawn.
"How long are you going to be cutting the grass?"
"The same length I always cut it."

In the world of invisible mending, nothing is as it seams.

Life is addictive but I wouldn't want to make a habit of it.

My wife was upset that I was late home from work. Question after question. In the end I said, stop grilling me, I am not a sausage.

"Monsignor, what are you doing with that holy water?"
"I am pouring it over a desecrated coconut."

"Doctor, I keep getting stabbing pains in my back. What should I do?"
"Stop working for Donald Trump."

The governor asked Steve McGarret to audition acts for a charity on the big island. A juggler finished his act.
"Okay Danno, book him."

Just Another Cheap And Tacky Old Joke Book

I saw a holiday postcard recently, that had a bald man on it, tapping his head, with the slogan underneath.
"I wish you were hair!"

I walked into a Yorkshire pub the other day. It had rubbishy knitted figures on the counter. I asked what they were and was told that they were Ilkley Moor bar tat.

Why is how you greet yourself, when you see your own reflection in a mirror, like a Greek cheese?
Because it is Halloumi!

Why is Mr Micawber's precarious financial position like a French phrase?
Reason debt.

Why is a paper figure unlikely to make a good surgeon?
Because he is not cut out for the job.

Frankenstein's monster has got a new job. He is still finding his feet though.

I went on a works outing recently. I didn't realise everybody knew I was gay.

When this guy said he wanted to knock my block off, I thought he meant rob the safe in my tower block, until he hit me.

I saw this gorgeous girl walking down the street but I couldn't work out her ethnicity.
"Chinese or Indian?" I asked.
"Fish and chips, if you're asking."

John Lennon was reborn as a haberdasher. He could be heard promoting his wares instore.
"Gloves, gloves, gloves. All you need are gloves - gloves are all your need."
"Do you know one in three people have dementia?"
"Thank God there are two of us then!"

"Billy, why are you crying? "
"Ma, we went guising and rang Mr Phillips door. He opened it, wearing an ice hockey mask and said-
"Trick or mistreat? "
"Mistreat?" I asked and then he hit me with a baseball bat! "

Is horse racing the only use of mathematics, where odds are even?

Are monks boys in the hood?

How do giants and dwarves greet each other when they meet?
"High there!"
"Low there! "

"Riker, my nose is bleeding again."
"I told you captain, don't pick hard."

If you remove the 'I' from married, are you marred by the experience?

If a gangster wants to kill his wife, does he put a silence-her on his gun?

What's another name for pigs in blankets?
Sleeping policeman.

We usually eat out at fast food restaurants but thought for a change we would try nouveaux cuisine. Looking down at our plates, we saw two small islands with a squiggle of sand between. My wife stared at her dish and I said
"I see a tall, dark stranger, who isn't going to get a tip."

Is an alien abduction in Germany, a herr raising event?

Just Another Cheap And Tacky Old Joke Book

My education was a disaster. I'm what you would call an Eton mess.

Some crooks decided to steal back jewellery that a superhero had stolen from them. In fact they agreed that Batman needed robbing.

A witch was in a ducking stool, when one of her inquisitors said
"You have a answered everything correctly so far - now here is your sodden death question..."

I separated two East Europeans who were fighting. They were Poles apart.

"I have just sat on a hotpoint."
"Washing machine or spin dryer?"
" Neither. A poker out of the fire. "

Two telepaths were talking.
"I hope you don't mind me saying this..."
"Yes I do actually. "

My granny died because she liked line dancing. A train hit her at sixty miles an hour.

A man was killed in a car crash recently, when a pair of legs ran out in front of him. A witness told the police, he thought that the driver had stopped for a swift half.

I asked my girlfriend if she'd like a roll in the hay. She said cheese or ham?

Into bondage? Money shortage? You could be strapped for cash!

My dog has gone from biting the hand that feeds it, to fighting the hand that beats it.

Where would you expect to find a crazy shopper? In-Sainsburys.
I bought an unexploded mine field. It cost me an arm and a leg.

Two musicians were caught fighting outside a concert hall. One was accused of trying to stave the other to death.
The cardinal wanted to promote a junior cleric, so he fired a canon.

The good thing about shopping at a ship's chandlers is that there is always a sail on.

I'm glad I followed in my father's footsteps. He lays mines for a living.

I lost my wife recently. Unfortunately she found her way home again.

I bumped into somebody the other day, when collecting my pension. I said
"Don't you remember me?"
"No."
"Thank God for that - I don't remember you either!"
The winter Olympics are really cool.

I am suffering from OCD. Observed Critical Difference.

Is politics figuring out the lie of the land.

If you steal a cobblers chair, will he be the last man standing?

There is a certain Hollywood actress, who is disappearing even as we speak. She is of course Faye Dunnaway.

"I visited Venice last week."
" St. Mark's Square? "
"Yes but his brother is hip"

If Britain leaves the common market, will it be a single or a double Maastrichtomy?

I saw a man feeding the pigeons the other day. I said filthy, dirty vermin. He replied, no need to be insulting, I had a bath last week.

If a monk falls in a muddy puddle, does he have a dirty habit he should be ashamed of?

Sitting Bill was invited to peace talks with the lying white eyes.
"Last time you cheated my people. This time I want my brother with me as a negotiator."
" Okay, what's his name? "
"Talking Bull."

The Beano decided to go upmarket by producing a cartoon strip of a famous Shakespearean play - Hamlet, Prince of Denmark, also known as Desperate Dane.

Just Another Cheap And Tacky Old Joke Book

This really is the end!

(By that I mean life is a joke and death is the punchline)

Just Another Cheap And Tacky Old Joke Book

Just Another Cheap And Tacky Old Joke Book

Just Another Cheap And Tacky Old Joke Book

Just Another Cheap And Tacky Old Joke Book

www.ingramcontent.com/pod-product-compliance
Lightning Source LLC
Chambersburg PA
CBHW050039080526
44586CB00014B/1378